My FAT is NOT a Flaw

TroJah Irby-Morgan

DEDICATION

To the girl who hates her fat body.
To the society who told her that big wasn't beautiful.
And to the plus positive community who dedicate their lives to
constantly prove society wrong.

CONTENTS

INTRODUCTION
FAT FOR REAL

They questioned why I wanted to write an entire book on such a negative topic. They asked I felt so strongly about the use of a word that makes people cringe when said in social settings. A word so hurtful it ignites feelings of hatred upon thousands of people every single day. A word so wicked that as of 2010, studies indicated a 66 percent increase in discrimination against fat people, some say making prevalence rates equivalent to those of racial discrimination.

A word so powerful that studies show obesity is strongly linked to depression. In fact in a study of more than 9,000 adults it was revealed that mood and anxiety disorders including depression were about 25 percent more common in obese people studied than the non-obese. The results appear in an issue of *Archives of General Psychiatry* by Dr. Gregory Simon, a researcher with Group Health Cooperative in Seattle.

A word so cruel that statistics on bullying are upsetting. In a recent national survey of overweight sixth graders, 24 percent of boys and 30 percent of girls surveyed experienced daily teasing, bullying, or rejection because of their size. The number doubles with overweight high school students—58 percent of boys and 63 percent of girls experienced daily teasing, bullying, or rejection because of their size. A word so fatal that those very people who have experienced bullying can or have fallen into depression. And we all know depression can lead to suicidal thoughts. It's obvious that this word is by far one of the most powerful words in the world. When misused, the word *fat* becomes a weapon--a weapon of mass destruction indeed.

It's most popular use is most certainly derogatory. The National Association for Fat Advancement (NAFA) calls it fat shaming." Ironically, some people try to use the method of fat shame as motivation. I guess the people using the term in this manner expect it to be a rude awakening or wake up call. Newsflash: we look in the mirror in the morning and notice the extra jelly that adorns our bodies in special places. And my mind continues to think, sarcastically of course, as if we didn't go to sleep with one boob resting under our arm and the other boob waving goodbye in the opposite direction. As if we don't know that our chins sometimes has a twin. Or we never realized that extra roll that pops out of the side of our bra. Then I thought: maybe we didn't get the memo that most plus size sections in the two stores that actually carry plus sizes in the United States are located in the back corner and sometimes in the basement.

Ah ha! Maybe they thought we were blind as fashions for the fuller figured woman become harder to find appealing."" Once, while shopping in a popular clothing store, I waved a dress resembling a moo moo in the air and asked everyone, "Is this my dress or my grandmother's curtains?" I don't know. Maybe they think we should feel bad because our jeans don't fit anymore after taking on the world's most important job of birthing a beautiful being. Humph. Now that's fat for real! Yup. I'm convinced. The people who use the term fat to harm others are obviously displeased with themselves and use this one three letter word to define our very existence. However, we have to understand that fat is a relative term. We are so much more than the accumulated material in our bodies as a result of consuming extra calories. Truth: the word fat is not even a proper adjective. The word fat in medical terms is actually weighed by lipids." Yes, your girl an A in anatomy and physiology. Truth: we're supposed to have a certain amount of fat on our bodies for various metabolic and structural functions.

As you read this book and support the movement I want you to understand that in no way, shape, form, or fashion am I stating that it is alright to be unhealthy. I know one of the first things the critics will ask is "why are you promoting obesity?" There's a huge misconception in the health community arguing that if we encourage people to love their bodies, we will inadvertently encourage obesity. Yes, being overweight can lead to many health problems. Some of these health problems are the leading silent killers in America. Excess body fat content can have severe implications. That is a fact. There are tons of statistics relating obesity to illness. While these statistics are staggering and the studies have proven them to be true, many times these same studies are conducted without factoring in other characteristics about the person. Take Joannie and Shameeka, for example. Here we have two completely different women from two completely different ethnic backgrounds (one is Caucasian and one is African-American) and different family histories. Yet they are both tested and judged by the same standards. Doctors believe if both women are the same height then both women should also be the same weight by a certain age. How fair is that? As a result of this medical standard, society believes there is only one way to be fat, one way to be skinny, one way to be fit, one way to be healthy, and of course, there's only one way to be beautiful. Thin does not mean healthy.

In the Middle Ages overweight women were considered beautiful. Today, many Afro-Caribbean and island cultures throughout the South Pacific still believe in the beauty of overweight women. It's important that as fat people, we understand that our health comes first. There is in fact a better way of living out there for us. Being fat and unhealthy is not alright. However being fat, having confidence, and living a healthy lifestyle is most important. And I want to put emphasis on the idea of finding what works for you. Everything does not work for everybody. Find your own balance. Try not to compare yourself to

other people when finding a healthier way of living. Your results
will not be their results. The premise of the Health at Every Size
(HAES) movement is to make people aware that weight does not
determine health. The purpose of the movement is also to stress
that exercise and good nutrition are beneficial, regardless of
whether or not they result in the loss of weight. Instead of using
that horrible body mass index chart, HAES advocates using more
specific measures, like blood pressure and cholesterol, to determine
one's health status. It's been proven time and time again that diets,
weight loss surgeries, and different methods of exercise show
different results for different people. Now that's fair! HAES
methods should be used globally.

On the other hand, a balanced lifestyle filled with good
nutritional habits, exercise, and mental stability will ensure a happy
and fulfilled life for anyone. We shouldn't have to feel pressured to
conform to what the world feels we should be. Studies show that
women will always wish to conform to the norm of their
naturalized society. It's just really unfortunate that in our Western
society people demand such perfection. We've been brainwashed
so badly that we've even come up with our very own dictionary of
words to avoid using the word fat. For some reason it makes us
feel better. It doesn't make the fact that we *are* fat sound so bad
when we use the elective words. Warning: what I'm about to say
may offend some people but this subject and therefore this book is
NOT for the faint of heart. This is FAT FOR REAL. It's what we
live; it's how we live, how we can become better and do better

beginning with ourselves. So, back to the words I like to call sugarshit. I call them sugarshit because they were solely created to make what society considers to be nasty (the word fat) sound sweet and desirable. For instance, instead of using the word *fat*, some ladies like to call themselves *thick*. Who wants to be labeled fat when they can call themselves thick? Thick sounds sexy, inviting, enticing, and desirable. Our minds have been so taunted with the word FAT that we now believe that FAT is like the ultimate sin. I'm here to tell you that being fat is not a death sentence. Being unhealthy is! Check out this list of words I've compiled that us fat girls like to use to describe ourselves these days:

• Thick	• Fluffy	• Big Girl
• Plus Size	• Voluptuous	• Brick House
• Bodacious	• Juicy	• Full Figured
• Big Boned	• BBW, SSBBW	• Heavyset
• Size Sexy	• Chunky	• Pleasantly Plump

And last but certainly not least, someone was creative enough to change the entire spelling of the word and made the letters as acronyms for other words. Remember this?

P.H.A.T (Pretty Hot And Tempting/Thick) I won't even touch on

6

that one. I'm moving on.

I can't lie. I absolutely LOVE to use some of these words because the truth is I TOO have been brainwashed into thinking they sound better then using the word Fat. But my rants and my passion behind becoming more comfortable with the term *fat* without offending someone else has come full circle. I do however believe some of the sugarshit words SHOULD be used in certain situations. For example, in the plus model world (runway, print, commercial, fit etc.) you wouldn't DARE label the model as a Fat or BBW model. The proper term is "plus model" or "plus size model." That's just Plus Model 101.

BBW, in case you weren't aware, stands for Big Beautiful Woman. This term is very popular within the "adult" plus community. The porn stars, strippers and fetish models frequently uses the acronym BBW or SSBBW (super-sized big beautiful woman). But these are just some of the terms we use to avoid saying the word Fat. Do you know that being Fat is idolized in other parts of the world? Excessive fatness continues to be embraced by many countries as a sign of health, wealth, and happiness.

According to toptenz.com here are the top ten countries that celebrate female obesity.

1. **Mauritania (West Africa)**
2. **Nauru (this South Pacific island has the highest rate of**

diabetes in the world)

3. Tahiti (French Polynesian island)

4. Afghanistan

5. South Africa

6. Samoa

7. Jamaica

8. Fiji Islands

9. Kuwait

10. Tonga Islands (South Pacific islands)

The bottom line is the use of the word does not become an issue until it is used in a context meant for hurtful purposes.

Furthermore it's not what they call you, but what you answer to. The purpose of this book is to entertain you while stimulating your mind as you develop conversational pieces about the use of the word *fat*. No more hiding behind the word. No more cringing when it's mentioned in a social setting or used inappropriately during water cooler conversations.

And if all else fails this book will definitely share personal experiences you can relate to as I take on life as a big girl in this small-minded world. I want you to complete this book knowing that you are not alone and someone has gone through similar situations when dealing with body conscious subjects. This book will uplift, encourage, empower, and also provide solutions on how you too can become more confident and comfortable with the term FAT. By the end of this book you WILL shout, "my fat is not a flaw." Remember you are beautifully and wonderfully made!

1
FAT BEGINNINGS

Thanks to the amazing advances of technology doctors can now determine if your baby will be fat or skinny. Well, you know what I mean. All sorts of test can be administered to the mom to be as well as the fetus for everything from gender and weight to illness and deformities. The mother to be tracks her babies growth each time she sees the doctor. The more pounds the fetus gains the fatter the baby will be once he makes his debut to the world. And of course when you come from a fat family, grandma and auntie always diagnose the baby. "Chile that baby gone be big as you," is what they'd say. Well, I don't know when my mom found out I was entirely too big for her belly, but I do know I was born nine pounds, nine and a half ounces. Some say I was destined for fatness. My maternal grandmother is five feet and weighs well over three hundred pounds. My grandmother on my dads side is five foot 8 two hundred pounds plus. All of my aunts and uncles are big. My mom is pleasantly plump (notice the "sugarshit") and my dad is over six feet tall two hundred pounds solid. So, it was pretty inevitable that I too joined the Klumps. Weird thing is none of my first cousins are fat. I'm the only one. Growing up I constantly asked God why me? I went through what I like to call the phases of fat. These are pivotal moments in your life when others neglect to find out who you are as a person. Instead, the people give you titles. They don't call you by your name. No, that would be too nice. And you can't be nice to the fat kid.

Early childhood days I was known as "the chubby one." Elementary days I was "the biggest one in the class." Middle school I was "the big girl with the pretty voice." High school I was "the big girl who can sing." College it was "the big girl with the pretty face and fat ass." It's tough being known as the "big girl" all of your life. For a long time it was as if I had no name. I wanted to be so many things and none of those things were "me." For some strange reason society believes most fat kids are bullies. Truth is, I was bullied. I had no brothers or sisters to come to my aid when being bullied. My dad was in and out of prison during my younger years so he couldn't really protect me. My mom worked so hard and as much as she tried and wanted to be there for me she couldn't because of her demanding careers. It had gotten so bad I never wanted to go outside during recess. If I did go outside I couldn't play in peace. I would try to jump rope and with every step I took the bullies would be surrounding me making BOMB sounds. If I try to run they would point, laugh and say things like "the Earth is shaking." As much as I wanted to eat I dreaded going into the cafeteria. Now don't get me wrong. I was very popular. Partially because I was always the biggest one in the class. Hell, I was a women's size 12 in the second grade. I remember my favorite pair of jeans were Calvin Klein. My family had lived in the neighborhood for years so if I wasn't being called one of my "fat titles" I was being called "Felecia's daughter", or "Hass' daughter." Adults in the community would step in to defend me because of the respect my parents had in the neighborhood. I appreciated that more than they knew. So, Gina, my color guard coach, ,Ms. Boatwright, Mr. Blackman and Mr. Harris, the security guards, Ms. Ester as well as anyone I may have neglected to mention, thank you. Thank God there were people who actually believed in me at such a young age. They saw something in me I never knew existed. They played very important roles in my life during my elementary school years by helping me believe in myself. I'm sure if you think back to some of the most painful moments in your life, you'll remember that one person who was always there for you. Even if while you're going through those times it seems as if you're all alone, you are not. The people I mentioned helped me realize the confidence inside of me. They helped me realize that I too was truly great and special, and worthy to do whatever I wanted to do with my life despite my size. So to Ms. Thomas-Keys, my first music teacher at Hawkins Street School, Ms. Jones, Dr. Strand, D'Juana Smith, Ms. Pugh, Ms. Joyce, for showing the class my fat was not a flaw in the 2nd grade by putting me over your lap and giving me birthday spankings. I felt included and the kids treated me nicer after that. I felt like you weren't afraid of me as the biggest kid in your class—thank you! Ms. Curry, Ms. Mack, and Ms. Ebony Mack-Ramos--you ladies groomed me into a pageant queen. I was the biggest contestant and you all made me a winner! You believed in me when I didn't believe in myself. Those

moments and lessons will live within me for the rest of my life. I
am forever grateful. I don't know if any of you will actually read
this book, but I'm shouting to the universe, THANK YOU ALL
FOR HELPING ME BECOME THE WOMAN I AM TODAY.
Wow! Until this very moment I never fully realized just how many
encouraging people I had around me all of my life. There were so
many times I felt so alone. Especially as an only child we tend to
have more alone time than others. Because of this, one thing I'll be
forever grateful for is how my mom kept me in extracurricular
activities. Once I started to accept the fact that I was indeed fat and
the fat wasn't going anywhere, any time soon, I indulged myself in
a number of activities. Truthfully, I participated in a lot of activities
not because I necessarily liked them—I wanted to prove to others
that I could do it too. In retrospect I realize that was my
motivation. I played basketball because as a big girl everyone
automatically assumed you had to play basketball or your size was
a waste. But honey me and basketball just couldn't be friends for
long. Those tight shorts kept riding up in my thighs and my jersey
was always too tight. I didn't like to sweat and most of all I hated
suicides. If you've never heard of suicides, please, count it a

blessing. Suicides is this ridiculous exercise ALL basketball players have to endure if they plan to stay on the team. I encourage you to "google" it. I even played soccer and won a trophy. Aside from that I was always doing something to enhance and showcase my musical talents.

Music is, has been, and will always be my first love. I honestly feel my talent saved my life. I saw what happened to other fat kids who were not accepted by their peers. The only thing that set me apart from other fat girls was my gift of voice. One minute the bullies would follow me home from school. And the next minute they'd be asking me to sing at their parents' funeral. I kid you not that is a true story! Growing up in the projects you see people getting jumped all of the time. I thank God no one ever had the guts to actually put their hands on me. But there were times when the words that spewed out of their mouths did more damage than a punch ever could. Sometimes I would wish they'd just beat me up already instead of standing around me and taking turns demolishing what little self-esteem I thought I possessed. I could remember running home and telling my mom about how bad other kids would pick on me. My mother would come downstairs with a bat in her hand and point them out asking me "who did it? She even said "if you don't hit them, then I'm gonna hit you!" Once she did that, no one wanted to fight me anymore. I do remember having this one fight and I hit the ringleader chick with a one hitter quitter and homegirl slid across the concrete pavement. She was six years older than me. I just got tired of living in my own community and not really being able to *live* in my own community. If that makes sense. It had gotten to the point that I felt like me being born fat and into a fat family was an automatic set up for failure. I would walk around with the ice grill on my face. While I'd still be polite to people I could remember going out with my mother and people would ask, "why she look so mean?" I heard that statement for years. They just didn't understand. It wasn't that I was a mean person; I just didn't want to look vulnerable and have people try to take advantage of me. On the inside I was a gentle giant. But I couldn't let my peers know that. After being bullied for so long and beating up one of the ring leaders I promised myself that wouldn't happen to me again. I didn't exactly know how I was going to prevent it but I then realized I had a little power after laying the smack down on ole girl's candy ass. But guess what happened? I too, became a bully.

I didn't even realize it. One of my closest friends pulled me to the side with one of our favorite teachers, Ms. Pugh, and cried her eyes out explaining that I had begun to treat her the same way the bullies used to treat me. And it broke my heart. She was my best friend. I now understand that my defense mechanism to being bullied was becoming one. You know what they say, "if you can't beat em, join em." But I knew that was not me. That was not the life God wanted me to live. And that was not the life I wanted to live. I didn't want people to be scared of me. I was already frowned upon for being fat so to have people think I'm going to attack them too was just double trouble. I ended up switching schools completely.

After taking a test I was accepted into the gifted and talented program at University High School. I entered the school as a seventh grader and that's when I began to realize my fat was not a flaw after all. Folks were eying my junk in da trunk and I got a lot of attention as the "stacked" new girl in the school. But that's not the kind of attention I wanted. In the seventh grade I was well on my way to being a brick house. I was already wearing a D cup bra and at least a 16 in my clothes. I was going to school with older students now so I wasn't the biggest, nor was I the baddest. I kind of, sort of, fit in. But you know, there's always ONE person that just have to test you. And of course, it's the littlest chick with the biggest mouth. All year long this little girl would call me all kinds of fat names. I ignored her the entire time. Finally on the last day of school I couldn't take it anymore. I dared her to call me another fat B*tch. And she did. BOOM. The fight began. Seventh grade fully developed ta-tas were everywhere. (this little girl had some big boobs too). Just my luck (or not) I had on timberland boots, sweatpants and a t-shirt that day, so I was ready. Oh what?. Did you say I intended to stomp a mud hole in her? No way, not me. To make a long story short she caught an asthma attack and had to go to the hospital and I was kicked out of the school. I know we all have the story of victory when we finally mustered up the courage to verbally or physically confront the bully. I may have gotten in trouble for the confrontation but it was the most liberating moment of my young life. And I'm not condoning violence, I'm just saying some folks just need to get popped in the mouth every now and then. No, but seriously. Bullying is a very huge topic in our society today. Children are killing themselves and others because of bullying. As a result, schools are taking on this issue more aggressively . It's important to talk to your children and loved ones about what to do if they are being bullied. I can tell you right now my family only gave me two choices:

1. All of my cousins wanted to go down to the schools and CLEAN HOUSE (which wasn't a good idea because the day after I'd be back alone again).

2. Do what my grandma said do, talk trash back! So, Grandma TuTu (my maternal grandmother) would tell me things like "Chile, when they call you fat just say:

- "You just mad because yo momma feed you hot dogs and pork & beans and my momma feed me steak."

- **"Don't get mad because you still have to shop in the** toddler section of the store."

- "Your just jealous because I can fit Victoria Secret bras and panties and you have to wear "young world training bras."

- "I'm fat but your ugly. I can lose the weight but you can't fix that face!"

I'm telling you, I remember some of her comebacks like it was yesterday. And when I had the courage, I tried them and they worked. Of course the bullies tried to say anything to hurt me, but once I got that little bit of ammunition to boost my confidence there wasn't NOTHING they could tell me. Sometimes all it takes is a little ammunition to fire up something great within you. For you that ammunition may not have been funny jokes from grandma. It could have been the comfort of the word of God as it says "he created us in his image." Or maybe it was your father who constantly reminded you that you were the prettiest princess in the world.

I know for me there was one thing my Grandma Brenda, my dad's mother, used to say to me when I would cry to her about being bullied. Her statement would stay with me forever in a number of different situations. She always told me (and still reminds me) "You have an eagle like spirit. During a storm birds fly in flocks and eagles fly above the storm alone." And I want to tell you that you are an eagle too. It's ok to be alone sometimes

because the truth is you are never alone. There is always someone

greater than you and he is watching our every move. He may not

come when you want him. But he's always on time.

2
I'M FAT?

We all have that one friend who is in denial that she is indeed

fat. She hangs around the smaller folks. She wears clothes that

skinny chicks wear. She says things like "Oh I don't really get along

with other big girls." Or she says "I'm not fat. I'm thick." She

constantly shops in stores that don't sell her size. She pretty much

does everything she can to avoid living the *fat* life. So if you've

never came across a friend like this, then she is probably you! She is

You! I'm just saying. Are you in fat denial?

Do you think your "cut from a different cloth?" Think you

have a lot in common with our skinny counterparts? Are you the type who don't really attend plus size events or big girl parties but you are constantly getting turned away from regular clubs because you look a wee bit different than all of the other party goers? I've got news for you honey. YOU ARE FAT! And ain't nothing wrong with that! Please don't get me wrong. I'm not saying because you are fat you should only hang around other fat people. I'm not saying you can't have skinny friends, but what I am saying is keep it real with yourself.

You try walking up a flight of stairs and by the time you get to the top you're out of breath. Yup, you're fat. You ever sit down at a table and try to cross your legs but find it a little difficult to do so? Yup, you are fat! Can't put on a pair of jeans without laying flat on your back on your bed to button them? Fat. You take off your bra and it feels like the weight of the world has just been lifted off of your shoulders. FAT! Do you have bootydo? You know, when your stomach pokes out more then your booty do?! Yup. Baby, you're fat! There I said it. And I ain't taking it back. Question: why do you feel so offended? Did I use the word fat too many times? Have I no right to recognize one when I see one? Am I being a little too harsh? Am I not politically correct? The funny thing is some women would rather be called the "B" word instead of being labeled as fat! They get into arguments with their boo thangs or their friends and can be called a female dog dozens of times. But as soon as someone says the infamous "F word" ya'll be ready to fight. What's up with that?

And I most certainly can't forget about the big girl who likes to hang around other big girls who are LARGER than her so she doesn't feel like the fat one in the group. Women are a hot mess sometimes. See that's the problem. We are too busy sugar coating the facts of life thinking it will make us feel better about ourselves. Confidence doesn't come when you master the art of manipulating yourself into believing you're not fat. Self-esteem isn't gained by finding ways around looking at your body or refusing to face yourself. Beauty isn't wearing a *Body Magic, Spanx, Magicsuit* or any other body armor contraption that will deceive you into believing that's what your body really looks like when all of that crap comes off. The truth is neither confidence, self-esteem, nor beauty can be defined by what you project in the mirror or in the sight of others.

Real beauty is the cellulite on your thighs, the scars from giving birth, and the extra skin that jiggles when you raise your hand. Real beauty is your larger nose and fuller lips. Real beauty is found in our flaws. Self-esteem is that feeling you get when you see an outfit and you know you can rock it like no one else. And confidence is going out to buy that outfit and putting it on knowing that you are beautiful in every way. Self-esteem is our internal feelings and having confidence is the outward expression of those feelings. Self-esteem is actually your ability to believe in yourself. It provides you with the idea that you can do anything. Having confidence is the action you take on your beliefs to actually do or be whatever and whoever you choose to be. While they go hand in hand there are plenty of women who have self-esteem but no confidence. People often say, "you have to come to grips with your weight and who you are." But when you say the phrase "come to grips" it sounds like you're trying to force yourself to accept something. Loving yourself and having confidence in yourself regardless of weight should not be forced. It should come naturally.

It shouldn't be that hard to embrace the skin that belongs to you. And truthfully, it's not that hard once you learn to ignore the common misconceptions existing in the world. It breaks my heart when I see perfectly healthy and beautiful curvy women hate their bodies. I can't say it enough. Being fat is NOT a death sentence. But being unhealthy is a death sentence. To the girls who just went through one of the most beautiful experiences on this Earth by giving birth and now you can't fit into your favorite pair of jeans, please know that you are beautiful. Those jeans do not define you. To the high school prom queen who now finds comfort in eating cookies and ice cream while studying for a test: please know that you are beautiful. To the girl who got offended when the retail specialist told her the store did not sell her size: know that their clothes were probably ugly anyway. There are now fabulous establishments on the internet as well as physical locations ready and willing to cater to you with open arms. Know that it's not about the *size* you wear. It's about how you *wear* your size. The moment you walk into your own truth about your body will be the defining moment of your entire life. The way you see you is what's most important. Most people can spot a fake a mile away. You can put on a face full of makeup, pull up your girdle, and wear 15 pounds of accessories and hide behind the big hair and a big bag if you want. But people can absolutely spot a mole. They know when you're not really about the life you pretend to live. The longer you wait to face the fear of yourself the longer it will take to truly enjoy life. And the truth is having built a high self-esteem and optimizing on your confidence will not be the end to your insecurities. You will always have your good and bad days. That's a little something we call life. It's not about how many times you get knocked down. It's about how many times you get back up. It's about the steps you'll take to push forward. Realizing and accepting your fat is not so bad. You can take it all in stride and flaunt your extra jelly or just do what my girl Tyra Banks did on her talk show a few years ago and shout to the world "KISS MY FAT ASS."

3
DREAM KILLER

Growing Up you had a dream. You dreamed of one day becoming so great that nothing and no one would be able to stop you. You knew in your heart that everyone would love you and you'd possess every single thing your heart desired. Yup. You and your dreams. Maybe you dreamed of being a doctor. A ballerina. A concert pianist. A police Officer. A judge. An author. A teacher. Or a business owner. Maybe you were like me. I used to dream of being a famous singer. That dream hasn't died yet. All I ever wanted to do was sing. I wanted to record albums and perform on stage. That is my dream. I believed when I was young that I WAS the next Whitney Houston, Mariah Carey, Faith Evans, and Jill Scott. Hell, I was the next Beyonce! That's right. I wanted to be the fifth member of Destiny's Child so bad. I wanted to wear the cute outfits, die my hair, and wear extensions. I wanted to dance on stage like nobody was watching and share my passion for music with the world. So why am I not a rich and famous singer? Why haven't I recorded hit songs and performed with some of the industry's greats? What stopped me from living out my dreams? ME!

As most people do, I got in my own way. We can sometimes be our own worst critic. Especially after we allow others to validate our insecurities. Forget "blaming it on the goose" as Jamie Foxx would say. "BLAME IT ON THE FAT!" There is no denying my God given talent. I' been told thousands of times that my voice was something special. I've witnessed the power of my voice first hand. There have been times when I sing and it was as if the audience was under my control and in some sort of trance. I had the power to make people smile, cheer, and burst into an uproar and even cry. I've had big time music executives tell me I had a voice better than

90 percent of the current artists who were hot and living the life I wanted. . So I would say to myself, and those execs, what is the problem? Why can't I get a record deal? Some would tell me flat out I was too big. And others would beat around the bush and say things like "you don't have the 'look' that sells." You know what they say, sex sells. But then they would add insult to injury by saying that infamous line: "you have a pretty face for a big girl." What do you mean I'm pretty for a big girl? Are big girls supposed to be ugly just because of our weight? Beauty doesn't have a weight limit! It amazes me to this very day how people can make such insensitive comments . I just never understood their logic. Truthfully, I still don't. Something special happens when I hit the stage. It's as if I have no weight or look. The people just hear my voice and judge me based upon my talent. The industry says no one wants to hear a big girl's story. They say no one will buy a fat girl's records. No one will purchase a ticket to see a plus size woman on stage. I know that's a crock of bull because most women in America are arguably a size twelve to fourteen. And that's just on average. So why wouldn't they want to hear music from someone they can relate to? Someone who looks like them.

Furthermore, I for one have felt the love I receive when I'm in front of an audience. And there are plenty of fuller figured artist out there doing the damn thing. Bad thing is they don't get the credit that they deserve. They don't get as much spotlight and attention as these no meat having, auto tune sounding, can't sing worth a split nickel pop and R&B stars the world idolizes today. I'm sure I don't need to name names. You all know exactly whom I'm talking about. On top of that, our plus size artists have to fight twice as hard to get the marketing, promotion, and publicity they deserve. I'm thankful to know that while they may not always get the credit that they are due they NEVER STOP and it gives me the strength to push forward.

From my fellow Newark natives Queen Latifah and Faith Evans to Jill Scott, Kelly Price, Ledisi, and Jasmine Sullivan to independent artists such as Storm Marrero and Rajdulari Barnes and others, I thank you.

Also I want to quickly address the ladies who came into the industry plus size and decided to lose their weight via surgery or by changing their lifestyle. Kelly Price, Jennifer Hudson, Monique, Jill

Scott, and Queen Latifah have lost weight. I hear a lot of people criticizing their decision to lose weight. Some say Monique and Jennifer Hudson are sell outs." I don't know your opinion on this matter but I wouldn't dare take away all that they have done for the fuller figured woman simply because they choose to lose weight. I think it's ridiculous that people are coming down so hard on them. At the end of the day it is their choice. We don't know why they lost the weight. It could have been due to medical reasons and the truth is it could have been that they were just tired of being fat! But don't get mad at them. Be happy for them. Be happy that they had the guts to accept the things they cannot change and they changed the things they can. Just because they are smaller does not mean they are any less talented than they were before the weight loss. Stop hating on them! Yeah, I said it!

In my journey within the music industry I was even told I wouldn't succeed in that industry *unless* I was a gospel artist. Can you believe they actually fixed their lips to tell me that the only way I would be a successful recording artist is if I became a gospel singer? I've even heard some say that fuller figured, light skin, pretty girls with amazing voices all do very well in the gospel genre because in the world of gospel they don't buy records based on your appearance. They buy records based on the message and inspiration. They must have lost their mind! Gospel music is not a backup plan for those who can't make it in the R&B world. It's not some leftover pile or misfits box. Singing the gospel is about a lifestyle. A lifestyle that you live when you decide to dedicate your life to Christ. And because I knew I was not at that point in my life I refused to even consider entering that world just for record sales. Are they crazy? So, here I am. Still singing every chance I get. In church on Sunday. Karaoke on Wednesday. Auditions, local talent shows, funerals, birthday parties, Bar Mitzvah celebrations, shoot, music is me! And although I do not have a record deal, God has still blessed me to be able to perform with some of the greats. I feel the love from people when I begin to sing yet my dream of being a famous singer has not come true—yet. For a long time I stopped dreaming about having a record deal. My insecurities got the best of me so I started focusing on other things that would protect me from being rejected. I was afraid to do a lot of the things I really wanted to do because of the fear of rejection. Truthfully, I almost stopped writing this book because I was afraid of being rejected. Every time I was rejected it seemed as if it was because of my weight. I didn't want to feel that pain any more and so I just stopped dreaming. I focused on reality, which wasn't always a pretty picture either. My fat had become my dream killer ya'll! It held me back from living the life I really wanted to live. I started to believe those executives and felt like I wasn't worthy enough to be a famous singer. No one wanted to see a fat girl on stage dancing and singing. The weird thing is, every single time I step in front of an audience and begin to sing, I know that is where I belong. I get a feeling that I've never felt anywhere else. It's a feeling I ONLY get when performing. So I'm now using other venues and resources to help me get back on track with my first love: MUSIC. I'm sharing this story with you to stress the importance of following your dreams no matter what. My weight got in the way and nearly wiped away every ounce of confidence I possessed. Don't allow your weight to crush your dreams. This may come to you as a surprise but one of my favorite songs is by the gospel group Mary Mary. I play it constantly when I need a boost of confidence! The hook to the song says "Go get it! Go get your blessings! It's your time!" Don't you know that IT'S YOUR TIME! Whatever your dream is, envision it. Believe in your dream. Plan your dream. Then execute your dream. What's a dream if you really don't believe it will come true? Take the time to research and invest in whatever it is you choose. Have a plan from start to finish. As my mom would say, "have a plan A, B, C, & D!" Then work hard on making your dreams a reality. And like I always say, "if you can't find an opportunity, make one!" When the going gets tough, the tough got to get going. The tough needs to move out of your way. Never give up something you can't go a day without thinking about! I challenge you today to dare to dream. Unlike many of us there are actually women out there who are afraid to dream. I know. It sounds crazy. But it's true. Maybe they are afraid of failure. They may even be afraid of success. Some may be afraid that it's too late. Whatever your dilemma, always remember that dreams can come true. But it's up to you. I can remember seeing my dad in the neighborhood and since I was never really the type to hang out in the streets I use to tell him "daddy I'm bored!" I used to get so upset when his response would be, "you are the author of your destiny, you are in control of your own happiness. Find something to do." But it was the truth. And that same statement applies to your dreams. You control your destiny. You are responsible for your own happiness. Keep God first in all that you do and everything else will follow. No matter how far fetched your dream may seem you have to believe with everything in you that your dream will become a reality. And remember it's never too late to dream. Whether you are nine, 29, or 59, you can always go after yours! Please believe me when I say your side gig (that dead end 9 to 5 job you work to pay bills and survive) is not the end of the road. Use it as a stepping-stone to move closer to your dreams. You are not stuck!

Not everyone will support your dreams. And that is alright. But you have to possess tunnel vision. Visualize going through a tunnel. First and foremost; you realize you can only move forward in a tunnel. You can't reverse and you are not allowed to change lanes. In order to reach our dreams we have to learn to stay in our lane. Do what works for you and don't focus on what others are doing. Just keep moving forward towards your destination. Also, when you think of a tunnel your goal is to always get through it.

The closer you are to the end the more you see the light. Be so focused on your end results and keep your blinders on to completely ignore the naysayers and the haters. You can't get mad at haters for doing their job. When I first entered the plus industry I was terrified of the opinions of my colleagues. Women are catty, drama-filled, and they can be very fake. Hey, let's call a spade a spade. They will tell you they support you, and even come to your event. Then, they will talk about you right after they leave. I've had girls who were on my team who gossiped about me and my business to other people. People I trusted. And of course it always hurt when its someone you care for or admire who is doing the bashing. But guess what? Start worrying when they stop talking about you. While it is very important to keep those people who support you very close, it is equally important to keep those people who are fakes, frauds, and phonies even closer. Now let's be clear: I don't mean be phony, be their friend, and hang out with them. I'm just saying keep your eye on them and do your best to stay a few steps ahead. People will pretend to rock with you and turn right around diss you. Trust me ladies. I know. I had a girl on my team who played nice for months. She pretended to be down for the cause. But she turned around and joined another team who hosted similar events. She talked about me with other people. She even talked about things that were discussed in our private group meetings with other people. Keep your eyes, ears, and your nose open ladies and be prepared to spot the moles. Because guess what? They are everywhere! People will pretend to be happy for you, ask you how you became successful, ask you for advice, and turn around and try to do the same thing you are doing. The world is filled with duplicators. But, in the words of model Jeannie Ferguson, when you become undeniable in what you do, there is nothing they can do to hurt you. Your real supporters and everyone else who watched you grind will know the real deal. I've realized that once other people—especially those who have been in the game longer than you-- begin to imitate what you are doing, it means you are doing something right! Oh and for the record: if you're reading this part and you think I'm talking about you, I probably am. But one thing is for certain: I don't do subliminal messages so I probably already told you how I feel about you. I'm just saying. Not to be nasty, or funny, it just is what it is. Those who mind don't matter and those who matter don't mind.

You will find that people you may look up to or reach out to for help will turn their nose up at you. Don't let it phase you. Keep pushing. Dream BIG! I keep my dreams in my pocket. No. Seriously. I walk around with a list of goals and dreams in my purse. The other day while updating my list of dreams I started writing a particular dream. Then I crossed it out. I thought to myself, "whom am I kidding? That will never happen." But then, God told me to rewrite my dream. And this time, write it in capital letters. I did just that! If you aren't afraid of your dreams, then you're doing something wrong.

4
THE LITTLE BLACK DOT

As an overweight child its inevitable that one day we would meet our maker during an activity that is supposed to be routine, we would come face to face with the devil . Now I'm not talking about spirituality and religion I'm talking about the little black dot. You've never heard of the little black dot? Well allow me to explain to you the responsibility of the little black dot and refresh your memory of that horrific moment your doctor told your mom that you were indeed fat!

Here's my story: my mom picked me up from school early.

I was just excited to be out of school early even if it was to go to the doctor's office. What made me even happier was to know that at the end of the doctor's appointment I was going to get a special treat. Yeah, you know the special treat! THAT DAMN LOLIPOP! So anyway, I'm at the doctor's office sitting in the chair just a swinging my little chubby legs. I run over to look at the fish tank as if I hadn't seen the thing a million times before. I try to play with other kids that are sitting there but my mom calls my name with that "come sit your ass down" tone of voice. I hurry to sit back down next to my mom with no hesitation because the kids were starting to pick on me anyway. Finally the lady comes out from the back holding a folder and screams out my name," TROJAN! TROJAN IRBY!" And the entire office giggles. Even though my mom would write my name in CAPTIAL LETTERS emphasizing the "H" on the end, these heffas would still call me "TROJAN." (Sorry, had a flashback for a moment)

In any event mom and I approach the nurse. Mom checks the nurse lady for saying my name wrong. The nurse apologizes and quickly seats us in one of the rooms. I'm forced to take my coat off and what's the first damn thing they make me do? Get weighed.

Ugh. I HATED getting weighed. They always seem to have a problem with putting that big piece in the right spot. All I could hear is "clink clink clink " as the nurse moved the piece back and forth trying to understand why this nine-year-old girl had more T&A than she did. Then she thought she was doing something wrong and tells me to take off my shoes and sweater only to find out she was off by one pound. She says "wow" as she wrote down my weight.

"Do I have to get a shot?"

"Nope," my mother says. "It's just a routine checkup." And it was definitely routine alright. Because after that day every single time I returned to the doctor's office, it was the same thing. Finally the doctor comes in and introduces himself.

"How many times does she eat a day," the doctor asks.

"Um every time I'm hungry," I interjected. "Duh."

"How many servings of vegetables do you eat everyday?"

"Who serves vegetables everyday?"

"How many cups of water do you drink per day," the doctor asks.

"As many as it takes to make some Kool Aid," I replied.

Listen my mom was not a huge cook. We were always eating out because she worked a lot and I had a lot of extracurricular activities. Don't ask us about a recipe because we couldn't help you. But ask us of a good place to eat and we've got you covered in just about any state up and down the east coast. Hold on though, my mom could make a mean pot of chicken and noodles, grits, and pepper steak and rice. Aside from that, she wasn't much of a cook.

Anyway back to the doctor's office.

As my mother tried to answer those questions the best way she knew, the doctor interrupts to give a warning on unhealthy eating. He then ask questions about other family members medical history. Once mom responds yes to all of the above and on both sides of the family, the doctor becomes alarmed and reaches for the infamous chart. I swear for some reason I could here the theme music to the *Twilight Zone* as the doctor reached behind the door to grab the chart of death. It is a very popular tool in the medical field to measure one's BMI and then tell you how much you should actually weigh. It's measured by your gender, age, and height. Your doctor takes his finger and follows the appropriate lines, skimming through the chart to find your little black dot. That dot is the mother of all health information. It is the bible for doctors and it's what they live by. They truly believe that by simply weighing someone based upon their gender, age, and height they should be able to know how much a person is suppose to weigh to be deemed healthy. That chart and those test were my worst enemy. I was insulted. How dare they base my being healthy upon a little stupid black dot? With those test and charts they never take into account other characteristics such as ethnicity, DNA, eating habits, or physical activity. Time and time again that routine check up became "routine". They'd check my weight, show me the chart, and tell my mom I need to loose weight but then become dumbfounded at the fact that I was as healthy as an ox. I never had any illness due to my weight. Even to this very day. I'd like to believe my activeness had a lot to do with that. I played basketball, soccer, was a member of a color guard, cheerleader, pep squad, jump rope squad, dance teams and so much more. I really wish that Kanye West song was out back then so when that doctor pulled out that stupid chart and showed me the little black dot I could just burst out and say "EXCUSE ME...IS YOU SAYING

SOMETHING? NAAAHH UHHHH YOU CAN'T TELL ME NOTHING!"

On the flip side there were a lot of young girls who did not take it all in stride. That little black dot taunted them throughout their entire life. They allowed that little black dot to define them. And if you think about it, maybe that little black dot wasn't on a chart. Maybe the little black dot was one of your closest friends who made a statement to you regarding your weight. Maybe the rude awakening came in the form of a loved one, or a time you went to the mall and couldn't fit a pair of jeans. Maybe your little black dot moment happened when you sought after your crush and they turned you down and said "I'm not into big girls." To this very day women allow what doctors, specialist, TV commercials, diets, and all kinds of things define who they are. Sometimes we fail to realize that there can be no change without acceptance first. How can you change an issue that you refuse to believe is there? It's impossible. That goes back to the topic of self-esteem and confidence. You can have all of the self-esteem in the world but without confidence your self-esteem is just puffs of smoke within you that you use to pump yourself up but never actually gain the confidence you need to actually make things happen. However you choose to make the change of losing weight the first step is to accept who you are. And I don't mean go around and downing yourself or putting yourself into a depression because you realize that you are fat or unhealthy. I'm talking about really truly accepting your body and loving it. A telltale sign of true body acceptance is when you can genuinely say "I love my body no matter what." Because guess what? You can have all of the weight loss surgeries in the world, do all of the Zumba you want, join as many gyms you want, and starve yourself to death by only drinking smoothies and juices but when those pounds begin to shed and your body begins to look different, guess who's still looking at you in the mirror? That's right! It's you. In your heart you have to love what God has created you to be because no one can do you better than you. Change begins in the mind and not the body. Once your mind is absolutely made up that you will love you completely and wholeheartedly with or without the weight your body will follow. Then and only then is when you can begin the path to making the physical change. Because at the end of the day once the weight is gone you're going to be stuck with a new figure and the same mentality of not liking or loving yourself. You'll still find reasons to beat yourself up and not be happy with your appearance. I know a lot of people who have lost a lot of weight. Some was due to stress. Some had surgeries. Others changed their lifestyle. But one thing a lot of them had in common was the neglect to change their thinking. One of my friends had a weight loss surgery but every time you turn around she's talking about food or talking about eating. Then gets mad because she can't eat the portions she used to eat. Or she notices the weight coming off but still has negative things to say about her changing body. To me that's torture. That shows me that she was not mentally ready for the journey she began with surgery. She was clearly getting what she wanted, which was to lose weight, but she still was not happy. That's because the problem wasn't with her weight. It was with her mind. She never truly had the confidence she needed to prepare for her new life. Her self-esteem was high. She knew it was something she wanted to do. She knew she was going to look awesome after losing the weight. But she never consulted with her mind first and fully understood what was getting ready to take place in her life. That goes for any person looking to make a change. Don't allow that little black dot to control your life. You are more than the little

black dot. You are more than the images our society idolizes as

beautiful. You are more than a quick fix. Don't you think you

deserve to be loved by you? Screw the love of others. What about

self love?

5
LOVING ME FAITHFULLY

"What's love got to do with it?" Only EVERYTHING! When it's all said and done, the big question is: can you look in the mirror and say with sincerity "I LOVE ME"? There was a time in my life when I didn't even want to look in the mirror let alone utter those words. I was so unhappy for so many different reasons. There was a time in my life when my fat was the least of my worries. My world was crumbling right before my very eyes as I entered a crucial period of my life. I was transitioning into high school and was very excited but nervous at the same time. In middle school I was always the biggest girl in class and I often wondered would things remain the same? I was accepted into the magnet high school of my choice, Arts High School, but I often dreaded going thinking I would be the only fat girl. Thank God I wasn't. I found my girl Tanisha Elijah! She was cute in the face and thick in the waist just like me. She had (and still has) the voice of an angle. We immediately clicked and she became my bff for most of my high school years. And I'm glad to say we are still cool to this very day. While I was transitioning into the high school life my mother was transitioning into a life of drugs. We lived in Hyatt Court projects in the Ironbound section of Newark, NJ.

Growing up, all of my friends' parents were strung out. My friends would always say things to me like "I wish your mom was my mom." Never in a million years did I or anyone who knew my mom, think she would become a drug addict. Yes, we lived in the projects, but when you walked into our apartment you would have thought you were walking into a condo. She always had the flyest cars and held a high paying job. She even worked at Newark City Hall while owning her own beauty salon for a while. I would always say my mom could have been president of the United States if she wanted to be. I won't go into too many details on how it all came about but one thing led to another and I found myself by myself. She was alive but her soul was dead. I could remember being home and not even knowing she was in her room all day long getting high. I felt like she chose the drugs and men over me. This added on to my low self-esteem. A lot of people in my life at that time had no clue what was going on behind closed doors. I've been working since the age of 13. I remember my mom stopped paying rent and I had to pay the rent at the age of 15. I can remember writing letters to my councilman and going down to city hall to speak with council members asking for help. And I received it too. I was born to hustle. My mom always had a hustle on top of a full time job. So this grinding lifestyle isn't new to me. Where was my dad you asked? He was around but he was heavily into the fast life and that was often his priority. He did what he knew how to do (when he wasn't in and out of jail) and I'm grateful because some kids grow up not even knowing who their father is. I felt so alone so many times. I swear if it wasn't for the prayers of my grandmother and the knowledge my mother had already instilled in me only God knows where and what I would be right now. The roles reversed and it was like I had become the parent and my mom became the child. I had to feed her with the lessons that she

taught me. I tried my best to love her unconditionally, but I was

already having trouble with loving myself. I was in a new school,

amongst new people. My body was already stacked and it was still

developing. I went through so many phases trying to find myself. I

needed my mom, but she was busy battling her own demons.

Another thing that kept my head above the ground was my talent.

Music saved my life!! I kept myself busy between school and after

school activities involving my music. Music was my escape. It's

what kept me going. Singing in front of people is what helped me

build my self-esteem. When I saw the reaction of an audience, it

made me feel accepted and loved. They didn't care about how

much I weighed. They didn't know my mom was addicted to drugs.

They didn't know I was a project chick. All they were concerned

about was my talent. Knowing that made me feel like someone

loved me for me. I felt equal to and sometimes better than others.

That's how much praise and accolades I would receive after

singing. It was my music and the encouraging words and prayers

from my saved sanctified and filled with the holy ghost

grandmother Brenda. And I can't forget all of the support from my church family Pentecost Inspirational Baptist Church. That's right. Even without my mom I went to church by myself. I would call Robin and she'd come and pick me up. I remember the church taking up offerings, then calling me up to the front and giving it to me. I didn't tell them I didn't have any money in my pocket. I didn't tell them my struggles with having to pay rent by myself. They blessed me over and over again and it always seemed to come right when I needed it. See my mother and my family already instilled in me the importance of having a relationship with God. I didn't know exactly what I was doing by going to church every Sunday alone but I knew I was doing something right. God kept me from dangers seen and unseen. That's what made me feel loved. These people saw something in me that I didn't see in myself. And shortly after that I was able to see the genius in me as well. I was able to love me FAITHFULLY. I'm no expert but I can share with you what worked for me to get me to the place of being able to love me faithfully. Before doing anything you must consult with God. Allow him to order your steps. Please understand that this was my process. I'm not saying what worked for me will work for you, but it is my hope that I am able to touch someone's life by sharing my process.

First you have to acknowledge the situation. Acknowledge the fact that you are fat. Acknowledge you are overweight or unhealthy. Acknowledge that you are indeed unhappy with the way things are going in your life. This is the hardest step but it is the most important step. It will allow you to see things for what they really are. No need to fool yourself. Stop playing games and open your eyes. The second thing I did was ACCEPT it. There's a mantra I learned while gong to an Narcotics Anonymous meeting with my mom years ago (who by the way is now seven years drug and alcohol free and working on earning her masters degree while holding two jobs within the behavioral health and human services fields. You can't tell me my God ain't real!). But while in this meeting the attics would recite the serenity prayer "God grant us the serenity to accept the things we cannot change, courage to change the things we can, and the wisdom to know the difference." But I like to personalize that sentence by saying "accept the things you cannot change, and change the things you can." The moment you understand that you were beautifully and wonderfully made and God has you right where he wants you to be, the acceptance process has officially begun. With acceptance comes freedom. Free of the pain others have caused you. Free of the pain you've caused yourself. Free of the worries of being accepted by others. And free of the worries of being judged by others. After you've gone through the acceptance phase you can finally exhale. The next step is a call to action. It's time to pull up your big girl panties and make some decisions. Will you accept what's going on in your life and stay the same? Or will you accept what's going on in your life and make a change? The ball is in your court. Remember you have the power. You can choose to change or you can choose to remain the same. Which leads me to the next step. CHANGE.

Girl if you are unhappy with your body, change the things you can. If you are unhappy with being fat lose the weight. If you are unhappy with your personal development conduct a self-evaluation. Change some of those character defects. Get counseling. The beauty of being a human being is the fact that we can evolve. It's up to us to seek the resources we need to make those changes. Don't think for one minute you can do it all on your own. Sometimes as women we allow our "superwoman-tude" to get in the way of us asking for help. We like to sip on the independent soup and shout to the rooftops "we got our own" and "we don't need anyone" mumbo jumbo. We all need support. And we all have someone that is willing to help us. Sometimes we chase them away. I know we sometimes get the feeling that we are all we got but that's simply not true. That person who's willing to support you may be right in front of you. Stop looking past them. Where there is a will, there is a way. And for every no there is a yes. You just have to continue to press. You never know who is willing to offer assistance until you've asked. I've built my entire brand through asking and bartering. When one person told me no I went harder and found two other people who told me yes. So just because you didn't get the answer you were looking for right away don't give up. A better answer may be just around the corner.

The last step is to WOOSAH and CELEBRATE! By now you've shed the tears, you've worked endlessly on changing whatever once made you unhappy . Now it's time to live and love a little. You don't have to go through life simply existing! It's time to

LIVE my dear. Go out on Friday and put your freakum dress. Get on that airplane you've been avoiding. Take that road trip you've been so hesitant to take. Wear a bathing suit on the beach. Fall in love!! Start your own business. Stop being afraid of taking risks and just do it! There is no need to be afraid of love. It's truly a beautiful thing. Love doesn't hurt. People do. You have to make sure you are giving your love to those who are worthy. YES WORHTY! Surround yourself with people who lift you up. Being confident in who you are and whose you are has everything to do with loving yourself and others. People will only do what you allow them to do to you. Don't even entertain the thought of being rejected or hurt. If you see something you want, go for it! In order to get the best you have to give the best and BE the best. Yes! You can be the best! My friends and I always talk about the importance of being the change we want to see. From our appearance to the way we treat others. Go on and say, "loving me. FAITHFULLY!" Repeat it every day. Loving yourself is a full time experience. You can't just love yourself when you have on cute clothes and a butt load of make up with a fresh new wig. You have to love yourself naked too! Remember "faith is the substance of things hoped for and the evidence of things unseen." So you may be unhappy with certain parts of your body but have faith in knowing that you are worthy of love. Self-love!

6
BIG SEXY

It has taken everything in my power to persuade myself to write this chapter without revealing too much information. I had to keep it real because if I decided to completely omit anything about sex in this book I'd be lying to my readers and myself. I promise I won't get too graphic and I don't want you to feel too uncomfortable while reading this chapter. I know this book may fall into the hands of a minor or some of my saved, sanctified, and filled with the Holy Ghost counterparts but at some point in life, sex is inevitable! Why not enjoy it? Yes, sex was intended for us to reproduce but it's also an opportunity to share an unspeakable passion with your mate. I was watching a documentary about South

African tribes who perform female circumcisions.

It is an age-old ritual where older women of the tribe cut the clitoris of little girls with a razor to prevent them from having sex for pleasure. It is their strong religious belief that women were put on this earth to simply reproduce. Let me remind you these tribes had no medical facilities to conduct these procedures. It's a sacred ceremony completed outside amongst a group of women and young girls. The girls are as young as two years old. After the procedure is finished, the poor babies can barely walk. The screams and pools of tears were unbearable for me. I almost turned the channel several times but I was too intrigued. To know that these girls are forced to make such a life altering change to their bodies to prevent them from feeling pleasure and stimulation during sexual intercourse absolutely was mind blowing.

Sex is your chance to express your love and passion for your mate through the movements of the body as you intertwine and exchange body fluids. Believe it or not, sex is a conversation without words. It's your moment to please and satisfy your mate in every way. But don't get it twisted. It's your time to release too.

Good sex relieves a ton of stress! When choosing to share your goodies don't forget that your mate has to bring the thunder too, honey. As big girls our low self-esteem tries to persuade us into thinking we should just take what we can get. No, no, no, my dear. Don't worry if he's not quite meeting the mark because if you are really into him and he's really into you, there are ways to make it work. You do know that you have the power to teach him exactly what you like. Right! Oh what? You don't know the power you posses? Girl, good vajayjay can pretty much get you anything you want from your mate. Trust me. I know. * **Evil grin** * Good vajayjay will stop a man dead in his tracks and keep him coming back. It will get you all of the material things you want. And I mention the word *material* for a reason. You can't expect to get more out of a relationship when it's solely based around sex.

Please do not abuse the power of the vajayjay. And don't think for one second that your good vajayjay is all you have to offer a relationship. Having good vajayjay won't make him love you darling. Your intelligence, your independence, your determination, and your heart will help him decide if you're worth keeping. What you have to offer the relationship will help him decide if you are wife material. Pay attention to the statement I just made. I said, WIFE material. Not WIFEY. Ladies, there is a difference. You don't need to be anyone's wifey. Wifey is the chick a man keeps around because she takes care of him like a wife is supposed to take care of her husband. However, if a man knows his woman is satisfied with being wifey, he'll never take that extra step to make it official and make her his wife. Yes, wifey may be first and foremost. Wifey may get the most attention and time. She comes before the rest of his jump offs. But a wife is his one and only. And you deserve to be someone's one and only. Not his first, second, or third. It sickens me to know there are countless full figured women whose self-esteem is so low that they become promiscuous and sleep with anyone who gives them a compliment.

I want to let you in on a little secret. Ok. Maybe it's not that much of a secret. But be careful out here ladies—men will use you! There are men who prey on plus size women with low self-esteem because they believe we will fall for any man who thinks we are attractive. Next thing you know we are paying their bills, buying their clothes, and moving their momma in! You have to really get to know the people you allow in your life. I know countless women who meet a guy and by the next month, they are living together. And ten years later, they are so content with their men and the ability to say, "I got a man at home." And they say these things even if their men are not worth one red nickel. You know sometimes we are so quick to scream "No, I don't want no scrubs" but we don't evaluate ourselves to try to figure out what we are doing to attract the scrubs. See, a man that only wants to use you for what you have, be it your money, your connections, or your body, will only approach you if he can spot your weakness. He will shred you into pieces by feeding off your weaknesses and you won't even know. A telltale sign your man is preying on your weakness is to watch what he says in the heat of an argument. If one of the first things he says to you during that heated moment is something hurtful or a shot taken towards your weakness or insecurity, then nine times out of ten he is using that as leverage and he is using it against you honey. Any man that truly loves you will NEVER use the things that hurt you the most against you. Yes, even in the heat of the moment. With age and experience, adults should know how to fight without hitting below the belt. There are plenty of ways to get your point across without taking jabs at the other person's insecurities. The sad thing is our crazy minds will make us believe he's just trying to "help." Or we say, "He loves me." Or we do whatever it takes to make ourselves, and others, believe that we are in love with him. Snap out of it woman! Don't you realize the power you are giving away?

Do you really think he loves you when he barely knows you? It is crucially important that you know your worth. Your body is precious. Your body is a temple. Stop giving these whack men owner benefits when they are just renting . Do you think by having sex with him it will keep him around? Sorry boo. You're wrong! The moment he gets bored, he's jumping to the next pretty face thick chick with low self-esteem. It hurts to hear this. Trust me I know. But using your body will only keep him, and you, satisfied temporarily. Once you've both climaxed, what else do you have to look forward to? Once that night of hot and heavy passion is all over what else can you all talk about? After engaging in such an intimate moment and taking that piece of you, the last thing he cares about is your favorite color. He doesn't want to know where you're from. He doesn't want to know about your family. And he could care less about some of your life's struggles. That's why it's important to share your most prized possession--your body--with the one who truly accepts and love you just the way you are. Flaws and all. The one who shows you he loves you better than he tells you. The one who grabs hold of those rolls you're so insecure about. The one who caresses your face without caring about how many chins you have. The one you can have sex with when the lights are on! That's right! WITH THE LIGHTS ON, BABY! And don't worry if you haven't found him yet-- God is preparing him just for you because the bible says, "he who findeth a wife findeth a good thing." And when you do find that special someone, make it your business to show him just who "big sexy" is. They say big girls are the biggest freaks. They say big girls do it better!

But don't get too hype now. Because they also say big girls are lazy and they think we all are pillow princesses. A pillow princess is someone who's not active in the bedroom. A pillow princess keeps her head as close to the pillow as possible. Come on now, ladies.

Stop allowing your weight to interfere with having amazing sex. Girl, we have more cushion for the pushing. We got more bust for the thrust! Ok. Ok. That was a corny line.

But seriously, it's important to keep it spicy. I've been there. Too afraid to get on top because I thought I was going to break "it." Countless times I've climbed on top and couldn't stop looking at his chest to make sure he was still breathing. I would keep asking, "Are you ok?" Not even realizing the more pressure I applied the more he became turned on. He would hold my hips and guide me to glory. In the beginning my legs would shake and I'd even lose my breath. These signs of being unhealthy *and* scared to death placed a fear in me. The fear of me being fat would take over and I wasn't able to indulge in the control and power I possessed while on top. You have the power ladies. Next time you are making love do the unexpected and climb on top. This drives him crazy! Make sure you switch it up. Dare I say it? "Bend over to the front and touch ya toes." Need some inspiration? There are plenty of adult films and pleasure items out there for you. Hey. I'm just saying. Explore your options ladies. Being "Big Sexy" is a secret lifestyle. Always remain a lady in the streets and a freak in the sheets. There's nothing wrong with being a freak for your man. Put something sexy on. Pop on Beyonce's "Dance for You!" Need help finding the right moves? Check out You Tube. There are plenty of twerking videos you can watch! Embrace your sexy. Men like women that are not afraid to take control in the bedroom.

Being sexy is not just about what you wear or how good your vajayjay is. It's a state of mind. Confidence is sexy. Intelligence is sexy. High self-esteem is sexy. Healthy is sexy. The way you carry yourself is sexy. The physical action of sex is just one small part of being sexy. And if you are not experienced don't worry because if your mate truly loves you he'll teach you what pleases him. You have to be open-minded. Sometimes we become so comfortable with our routine that we develop a fear of the unknown. How do you know you don't like something if you never try it? I'm all for experimenting. But only do so if you're really ready because you don't have to do anything that makes you uncomfortable. And if your mate tries to make you feel guilty about not wanting to try new things, then he is not the one for you. If he truly loves you he will respect you and your feelings. Just remember that what you won't do, someone else will. Believe That! On the flip side, having confidence in the bedroom is very important for both partners. Ladies you want them to make you feel comfortable, attractive, sexy, and wanted. Remember you also have to make him feel all of those things as well. There's nothing worse than a man with low self-esteem in the bedroom. Boost his adrenaline. Make him feel like he is the king of the castle. How? Next time don't wait for him to initiate a night of passion. You make the first move. Give him one of the juiciest kisses and ask him, "how do you want it?" There's nothing wrong with being submissive. Yes. I said submissive. Or if you want to switch things up and take full control go for it! Foreplay is very important. Massages are a great way to get him in the mood. Or take a shower together. I don't know but there's something about watching the water drip down my husband's naked body that drives me insane. Woosah! Ok. I'm sorry. I'll keep it cute. But you get my drift right? Open your mind ladies. Think outside the box. And please start having sex in other places besides the bedroom. My husband and me have this secret phrase we like to use. You may have heard it in an old rap song. It's called "the spontaneous express." That means it's about to go down right then and there. Now I'm not saying we have or have not had sex in different places but ladies, don't be afraid to ride the spontaneous express. Step outside the comfort zone you call the bedroom. Try the bathroom, living room, kitchen counter, or the washing machine during the spin cycle. Step outside on the patio. In the park. On a beach. A rooftop. Or on the hood of your car. What you looking at? You'd be surprised at how many different positions your fat body can morph into. Give it a chance. Tap into your sexy. Then unleash that bad boy. The curves on your body will only give him more to love and more to grab on to. Throw it back, drop it low, and touch the floor. You can do it! Believe in yourself. Believe in your sexy. I am Big Sexy. You are Big Sexy. Be big and damn it, BE SEXY!

7
STOP HIDING

In the dictionary the word *hide* means to conceal from sight.
So I pose this question: do you hide? Now when I say *hiding* I'm
not referring to the act of keeping yourself away from the public or
being antisocial because you are ashamed of your body. But when I
ask if you are *hiding*, I was referring to you hiding subconsciously. It
is very common for plus size women or any woman with body
image issues to hide behind things that we may feel make us
beautiful or more attractive. And this may not apply to ALL plus
size women so please don't start sending me the hate mail and the
Facebook inboxes talking about "not every big girl is insecure or
unhappy with her body." Right now I'm talking to those women

who find comfort in making material items her source of confidence. Some of us use items as our scapegoat to take the attention away from our fat bodies. I am guilty of doing this as well. Sometimes we hide behind baggy clothes. We try our best to get clothes not too snug on our bodies because we are simply unhappy with the shape of our voluptuous temple. Sometimes we are afraid to wear certain things because we feel like our rolls will show too much, or our belly will poke out too much or our booty won't look right. There are so many different style of clothes made just for our bodacious bodies. Understand that you too can be the fly girl walking down the street turning heads. Don't allow your weight to hinder you from wearing clothes that compliment your curves. Don't be afraid of color either! I know so many beautiful plus size girls who only wear black or dark colors. What's up with that? It be eighty degree's outside and ya'll be dressed in black. And when we see those ladies what's the first thing that comes to mind? "She know she hot!" Right! Another thing, don't be afraid of prints. There are all sorts of prints on fabulous and trendy pieces made just for us, honey. Animal prints, floral prints, abstract prints, and galaxy prints. Even this new beetle-juice (black and white) print everyone is raving about. Shop around, figure out your body type, and dress yourself accordingly.

Generally speaking there are five body types. You have the *pear, inverted triangle, hourglass, apple,* and *rectangle.*

The pear shaped body has a smaller top and wider bottom. If this is your body type try wearing shirts that will take the attention off your bottom and bring it to the top with boat neck shaped tops, ruffles, and bright colors. Also, try wearing darker colors on the bottom to create a slimming effect.

The inverted triangle shaped body has a large bust with narrow hips. This shape is the opposite of the pear shape. Therefore you want to draw attention to your bottom instead of your top. Don't be afraid to wear prints on the bottom half of your body. Also pleated and tiered skirts will take some of the attention off of your "girls."

The hourglass shaped body can be very curvy having a full bust, small waist, and full bottom. A wrap dress would be ideal for an hourglass figure. It's sexy and classy.

Now the apple shaped body is a rounder and fuller figure. When dressing an apple shaped body your goal is to create a shape. Try wearing flowy fabrics like chiffon and silk. In addition, high low dresses are great for the apple shaped body.

Lastly if you have a rectangular shaped body, your shoulders, waist, and hips are all the same width. Your best friend is a BELT!! It helps create a waistline. Asymmetrical hemlines will work wonders for you and if all else fails, try a peplum, which looks great on just about everyone.

Bottom line: try something different. Now on the other hand some of you "stacked" mamas hide behind very risqué and revealing clothing. You profess that you love the skin you're in and are not afraid to show it off. But just because you're showing skin does not mean you are *not* hiding. You could simply be causing a distraction by dressing super sexy. Maybe you feel like the only thing you can offer the world is your bootylicious figure. Then you wonder why every man you "bag" you can't keep. Oops. Did I just say that? You are worth more than that hun. You are a queen. Who wants to buy the cow when they are getting the milk for free? Old but true statement. You don't need to dress provocatively all of the time to prove you are sexy. Sexy clothes and attention from loser men will never fulfill the emptiness you feel inside. STOP HIDING.

Another thing we tend to hide behind is our hair. I salute all of you natural girls for rocking your God given manes. We spend way too much money on our hair. We get it fried, died, and laid to the side, boo boo. You know we do! But sometimes we use our hair to hide behind our insecurities. Lots of us fluffy gals like to rock the Aaliyah swoop bangs. You know what I'm talking about. The hairstyle with the one side covering the eye. You make yourself believe that if you cover half of your face it will look thinner. I'm telling you. I know ALL of the tricks! And my husband can't stand when I cover my big pretty face with hair. But what are you hiding for? What are WE hiding for? Show that pretty fat, chunky, chubby, double chinned face. You are beautiful. Oh! And let's not forget those of us who wear the BIG hair. Yes, hunni. I LIVE for big hair and a big bag. That's the Jersey Girl in me. A few years ago radio and television host Wendy Williams made a statement that always sticks in my mind. She said "the bigger the hair, the smaller the hips." I've come to realize and accept that it's nothing but an allusion. But seriously. The only people we are kidding is the person looking back at us in the mirror. We don't need to hide behind the hair. Rock it because it's an addition to your beauty. It does not make you beautiful!

And the same thing goes for makeup. I know plenty of ladies both big and small who won't pick up their Chinese food delivery without their makeup on. It's sad. I've heard through the grapevine that some of you "beat face divas" (ladies whose makeup is flawless), won't even allow your MATE to see you without makeup on. Even in the bedroom! What type of foolishness is that? When I'm ready to get it in with my husband, the last thing I'm thinking about is eyelashes and lip-gloss! You have to learn how to love yourself underneath the cosmetics just as much as you do with your makeup applied. Again, there is absolutely nothing wrong with wearing makeup. However makeup was created to enhance our beauty. Some of you may not like what I'm about to say but you are kidding yourselves if you expect people to believe you are flawless.

Our flaws are what make us beautiful. Perfect example: while browsing a friend's Facebook photos I noticed all of her pictures were absolutely gorgeous. She's a makeup artist and her face was BEAT TO LIFE! However I noticed two things. First, she only took pictures from the neck up. What's up with that? There are a lot of you ladies out there screaming "I love my body," I'm curvy and confident" as well as "I love the skin I'm in," but you only take pictures from the neck up! STOP FRONTING FOLKS! If you truly love the skin you are in, why hide your body? Take more full body shots. Get your pose on in the mirror or jump in those candid shots with your friends. There's nothing to be ashamed of, boo. The second thing I noticed I just had to share with my husband. I continued to browse her photos and found only one photo of her without makeup. I put the two pictures of this young lady side by side. The one with makeup and the one without. Do you know how hard it was for me to convince my husband that they were the same person? Ladies, makeup shouldn't have you looking like someone totally different. You wear makeup so much and so often that you actually begin to believe that's what you really look like. Know that you are beautiful with or without makeup.

And we can't forget the ladies who don't wear make up at all.
Why not? There's nothing wrong with getting dolled up. You
deserve it. It's awesome that you embrace your natural self but
baby, put some gloss on those ashy lips sometimes. Yeah, I said it!

The more I am introduced to successful women the more my
circle becomes full of single, "career-driven", sometimes lonely
women. There are so many women who hide behind your careers.
You run around like a chicken with your head cut off constantly
burying yourself in your work. I hear a lot of people professing that
"money is their motivator". It's a hard pill to swallow and I think
it's pretty sad. You mean to tell me of all the beautiful things life
has to offer the only thing that motivates you is money? Yes being
financially stable is important however it is not everything. I ache
for some of you women who wake up to the same routine every
single day.

*** Alarm goes off. You jump out of bed. Take a shower.
Get dressed. Grab your cup of joe. Pet and feed whiskers
(your cat). Grab your lunch bag and head to work. You come
home and do it all over again. ***

Ok! Maybe I'm over exaggerating and maybe I watch too much lifetime. But I know dozens of women who indulge in work and rarely make time for herself. Then some of you actually take the work home. I know I'm guilty of that. But we must learn how to work that nine to five and when its time to clock out...we really need to CLOCK OUT! Physically and mentally. Sometimes we can be so far away from work and still be thinking about what needs to be done when we return to the office. Have you answered your personal phone with the same greeting you use on the job? Don't laugh! I've done it! We all do it. But its just another indication that we must learn how to clock out mentally. There are actually women who never got a chance to LIVE. They are so focused on work, and their career when their entire life has become a routine based around their place of employment. This issue has become so critical that women are completely annihilating their social and love lives. Some wouldn't know what "fun" was if it came in a box that said "Krispy Kreme". Please ladies. Begin to live a little. Stop hiding behind dollar signs because when its all over you can't take it with you.

Now let's change the scenery a little bit. It's 90 degrees. You're on Miami Beach. You're ready to dive in the refreshing waters. You begin to take off your awesome accessories—big shades and a huge floppy hat before taking off your clothes and revealing your thickness. But in the blink of an eye you reach into your beach bag and pull out a heavy white t-shirt or swimsuit cover before diving into the water. Why must we hide in our bathing suits? I can't stand seeing my beautiful thick girls at the beach or the pool coming out of the water in a soaking wet t-shirt. Yes, we are fat. Yes, our thighs are chunkier and they rub together sometimes. Yes, our arms jiggle when we wave. God just gave us more to love. Don't think you must cover up because you are fat. The choice is yours because people are going to look and stare regardless. Truth is some will look at you in admiration wondering how you have the confidence and boldness to flaunt your thick body. And others won't like what they see. And you have to be ok with that. Either way I like to say, "love me or hate me, its still an obsession." The freedom comes when your able to be so comfortable in your skin that you don't even think about the opinions of others. Don't be intimidated by your smaller friends or the other girls gracing the beach in their bikinis. Go and grab you a Fatkini and walk in the sand with your head held high. Your body is alluring, dazzling, appealing, and grand. Own it. So the next time you're at the pool, or on that beach with your girlfriends, leave the white t-shirt in the bag. Let the sun kiss your skin. Of course with confidence comes responsibility. If you do plan on wearing a bathing suite please be sure to purchase your correct size. I'm tired of seeing you with your bathing suits up your booty and your boobies popping out every time you dip under water. Be sure to get bathing suits that fully cover your special parts. While we want to exemplify confidence we also want to exemplify class. They go hand in hand. I'm all for being sexy but there is a difference between sexy and trashy. Because of our weight people already label us as trash, unequal, low-class, and of course, lazy. The way we dress, the way we carry ourselves, and the way we live our lives is our opportunity to prove society wrong. We don't need to give them any more ammunition to fire their bullets. Stop giving them fuel to keep the fire going.

I want to rewind a little bit back to a statement I made a little earlier about hiding behind our friends. Why do we feel the need to hide behind the shadow of our *prettier* or *smaller* friends? My elementary school principal, Mr. Rindero used to remind students every morning "you are second to none." So I want to pass that on to you. You don't have to be the big girl playing your part in the background. You are just as beautiful and you deserve to shine, too. Same thing goes with our spouses or mates. We sometimes feel inferior because they may make more money or may be more outspoken and more social than we are. I don't believe in the saying "behind every good man there's a good woman." No. I believe beside every good man is a great woman." Ladies your partner would never make you feel less than. They would never encourage you to play the background. I know a couple that has this problem. Both are big people. Both are attractive. However, the man feels like his woman should be neither seen nor heard. He doesn't want her on social networks and he barely allows her to go out. To me this only shows his insecurities. A man is supposed to be present to lift you up and be a source of encouragement. A man needs to be your strength in areas you are weak. So to all of my confident, beautiful, curvaceous cuties, stop hiding. Come out! Come out wherever you are!

8

A WORK OF ART

"Why did you make me black Lord?

Lord...why did you make me black?

Why did you make someone the world would hold back?

Black is the color of dirty clothes, of grimy hands and feet...

Black is the color of darkness, of tired beaten streets...

Why did you give me thick lips, a broad nose, and kinky hair?

Why did you create someone who receives the hated stare?

Black is the color of the bruised eye when someone gets hurt...

Black is the color of darkness; black is the color of dirt.

Why is my bone structure so thick, my hips and cheeks so high?

Why are my eyes brown and not the color of the sky?

Why do people think I'm useless?

How come I feel so used?

Why do people see my skin and think I should be abused?

Lord, I just don't understand...What is it about my skin?

Why is it some people want to hate me

and not know the person within?

Black is what people are "labeled"

when others want to keep them away...

Black is the color of shadows cast...

Black is the end of the day.

Lord you know my own people mistreat me,

and you know this just ain't right...

They don't like my hair, they don't like my skin,

as they say I'm too dark or too light!

Lord, don't you think it's time to make a change?

Why don't you redo creation and make everyone the same?

GOD'S REPLY:

Why did I make you black?

Why did I make you black?

I made you in the color of coal

from which beautiful diamonds are formed...

I made you in the color of oil,

the black gold which keeps people warm.

Your color is the same as the rich dark soil

that grows the food you need...

Your color is the same as the black stallion and panther, oh what majestic creatures in deed!

All colors of the heavenly rainbow

can be found throughout every nation...

When all these colors are blended,

you may become my greatest creation!

Your hair is the texture of lamb's wool,

such a beautiful creature is he...

I am the Shepard who watches them, I always watch over thee!

You are the color of the midnight sky,

I put stars glittered in your eyes...

There's a beautiful smile hidden behind you

that's why your cheeks are so high.

You are the color of dark clouds

from the hurricanes I create in September...

I made your lips so full and thick,

so when you kiss... they will remember!

Your stature is strong, your bone structure is thick to withstand the burdens of time...

The reflection you see in the mirror,

that image that looks back...that is MINE!

So get off our knees,

Look in the mirror and tell me what you see.

I didn't make you in the image of darkness, I made you in the image of me!"

AUTHOR UNKNOWN

This poem "Why Did You Make Me Black Lord?" is from the perspective of a young woman who questions God about her physical appearance, particularly the color of her skin. She goes into detail asking about her full lips and hips and her coarse hair. The poem ends with God's response—he created us all in the likeliness of Him. One of my favorite lines is within God's reply when he says "your stature is strong and your bone structure thick to withstand the burdens of time. That reflection you see in the mirror...the image that looks back...is mine." I mention this poem because it tells a story of how special we all are. How many times have you questioned God about why he created you? This poem goes into detail about how God created us individually in his own image. I don't know about you, but I've been there time and time again. Asking God why am I fat? Why did I have to be overweight?

Why couldn't I be "normal"? I laugh about it now. First of all I can't even believe I had the courage to question God after all he's done for me. But when you really sit and think about it, he took his time to sculpt and mold us into a work of art. Art is the expression or application of creative skill and imagination, typically in visual form. Our bodies are visual expressions of God. No matter how fat, black, light, red, skinny, bald, short, or tall, remember there is no one on this earth made exactly the same. Art is one of a kind. We are one of a kind. Art is to be appreciated. We too, are to be appreciated. Our chubby faces, wide hips, thick thighs, big feet, jiggly arms, stubby toes, fat fingers, butter roll stomach, and hot dog necks are a part of who we are. But it does not *define* who we are. Please understand there is a difference.

I don't know about you but I do my very best to live this life understanding and accepting my purpose. And all I can do is suggest you do the same. Remember that all great achievements require time. And being confident in your own skin, accepting life's woes and learning how to dance in the rain is truly a great achievement. Let me explain something to you: our bodies are gifts. If you think about it, some gifts we fall in love with at first

sight while others we learn to love as it gains sentimental value.

We've all been on both sides of the spectrum at some point in our

lives. Hell, I'm not always content with the way my body looks. But

the bottom line is: it's mine! It's healthy; functions well, and can do

some things that can make you say hmm!! In writing this book my

purpose is to help you see the beauty of your fuller figure, help you

become aware of a few important statistics, and provide you with

strategies on how you too can be comfortable with the word FAT.

Being a big girl all of my life and trying to keep up with everything

plus size, I've realized that not all women are overweight because

they choose to live unhealthy lives. Now don't get me wrong.

There are plenty of women out here who simply do not care about

being fat. They are living an unhealthy lifestyle and choose to be

overweight and have handicapped themselves. Just today I was in

an office and a lady who was five foot two and weighing about

three hundred pounds said her doctor always reprimands her about

her weight. The woman bragged to others about her reaction—she

laughs in the doctor's face and then leaves the office, eating

anything she can get her hands on. Then she had the nerve to ask me, "do you feel me sis?" I kindly replied "no. No I don't feel you." She looked at me like I was crazy. To make matters worse the woman was pushing fifty years old. Now ladies you know it gets harder to lose weight and break out of habits, as we get older. She was really boasting about how all of her tests—blood pressure, diabetes, and others—came back negative. Yet, she couldn't finish a sentence without running out of breath.

I realize that every woman is not like that woman I encountered. Some of us get fat after a baby. We go to put on that pair of "old faithful" jeans and our world comes crashing down when we realize we can't fasten the buttons. There are women with ovarian cysts. Others have problems with their livers and kidneys. While some women have heart disease. All of these ailments can cause weight gain. And lets not forget the ladies who take birth control medication—it's easy to gain weight while taking contraception. I've noticed that you girls are the hardest on yourselves. All of you who don't really have any control over your weight gain seem to beat yourself up the most. Your new body isn't a curse. It's a gift. Treat it as such. Wrap it up tight and keep it protected. Only share your gift with those who are worthy of appreciating a work of art.

A masterpiece indeed.

9
FAT + FABULOUS= FATABULOUS

After all is said and done, you are left alone with your own

conscious . It's a fact that we are our own worst critics. But when

will we stop finding the need to over analyze ourselves? It is our

thoughts that provoke emotions and our emotions that provoke

action. Our actions will then determine how others react. We all

know the basic laws of the land. "For every action there is a

reaction." The question is: what is provoking our actions? It is so

important to remain mentally grounded, because the moment you

allow others to mess with your mind, your emotions will get the

best of you causing you to act up and act out The word fat is only a descriptive word. It is not the descriptive of you! Fat means plentiful or an "excess of." So what your plentiful happens to be measured in pounds! That's ok! I can write pages and pages of reasons to love your fat body until I'm blue in the face. But it would all be in vain if something doesn't click inside of you, to help you believe it deep down in your heart. What will it take for the light bulb to flash in your head? When will you experience your aha moment? Don't wait to loose weight because you hate your body shape. Lose weight because you are confident enough to know you are beautiful and sexy at any size. But being healthy is what's most important. WE ARE FAT! Yes, our abundance is measured in pounds! But think of it this way: having more pounds gives us a larger canvas for the curious to admire, honey! It is your opportunity and responsibility to display what real size beauty looks like. You are fabulous! In the words of Kenya Moore, you are "gone with the wind fabulous!" With the advancement of fat fashion, also known as plus size fashion, you too can look like you belong on someone's runway. As my girl Cassandra, owner of the hot plus boutique, Curvaceous Boutique in Virginia, says "make everyday your runway!" I run into so many women asking questions like "how do you have the guts to wear that dress?" I say "look down boo! You have a lot of gut too!" ROFL! Well you most certainly have the space for some! Look, I'm just being real. We already talked about the array of plus trends that are out there. Be FAT and always be FABULOUS . Be FATABULOUS! It's a real easy equation for those of you who don't like math.

Fat + Fabulous = FATABULOUS

Show the world you can be both! Even if you can't afford expensive things. Being fabulous does not have a price tag. I've rocked the mess out of dress or two from Wal-Mart. Being fabulous is also embodied in your confidence. Being fabulous no, excuse me...FATABULOUS is about daring to be different. It's about living out loud and experimenting to see what life, love, and happiness has to offer you. Yes ladies--we can have all three at the same time. But it's up to you to take the first step towards living a FATABULOUS life. Always remember that you are more than a conqueror. You are more than a pretty face, big behind, and juicy figure. Your fat is not your flaw. It's an enhancement!

My FAT is NOT a Flaw

PERSONAL ACKNOWLEDGMENTS

Thanking God first is not just formality. For I know that without
God I am nothing and through him I can truly do all things
because he is my strength. I learned at a very early age that there is
power in the name of Jesus and during my journey, I know he's
been on my mainline.

To my amazing husband Shameek Nashawn Morgan: there is one
thing in my life that I've never questioned and that is your love for
me. God sent you to me when I started to lose hope when it came
to love. It seemed like everything I loved let me down. Even my
own self-love was playing tricks on me. I wasn't looking for love.
Especially not a romantic love. But God used you to teach me how
to love. Not just others but myself first. The purpose you added to
my life was so unexpected yet needed. And I give nobody but God
the credit for creating you just for me. As I continue to grow and
evolve as a woman, a wife, a mother, and businesswoman I pray
God continues to give you the patience, support, love, and care
that I need from you, my husband. And I pray he continues to
provide me with the tools needed to always put you first and treat
you like a king. You are always so supportive in everything that I
do and I just want to take this moment to say thank you from the
bottom of my heart.

I love you, Mr. Morgan!

To my roots: Felecia Simmons Crute, I couldn't have asked God
for a better mother if I was there sitting with him as he was
creating you. I want you to know that the morals and values that

you have instilled in me I will forever cherish. You and I have been through so much together. But one thing that has never wavered is our mother and daughter relationship. That is sealed tightly! Even when people questioned your parenting you stood your ground and you did what you thought was best. They told you not to allow me to speak my mind. They told you not to encourage me to eat what I wanted. They encouraged you to cut me loose after a certain age. And now look at God. Because you did the opposite of what they said I am the beautiful, confident, outspoken, and full figured, independent woman I am today. No one can take that away from you. I want you to know that your job is done. Soon and very soon you won't have to work another day in your life. Between your two grandsons and me you are going to be well taken care of. Everything I know. Everything I do. Everything I am I owe it all to you. Thank you for investing your life into me. I love you mommy! To my first love: Marcus Raymond Irby. Daddy, you were my first example of true love from a man. I want you to know that no one will EVER be able to take that away from you. Knowing the life you lived as I was growing up I can confidently say you did your best in participating in my life. There were plenty of moments I was so disappointed in you during my adolescent years but I can truly say that our good times most certainly outweigh the not so good times. In my adult life you play such a crucial role. When you're not around I feel like my lifeline has been cut. No matter how big I get, how old I get, how "important" I become, how many titles I may earn, I want you to know that I will ALWAYS be daddy's little girl! I love you, daddy!!!

To the pieces of me, my sons: Jahmeek Raymond Morgan and Josiah Anton Morgan. I want you both to know that there is NOTHING too hard for God. I want you to always keep him first and remember his word (above all others) will forever remain true. When people tell you no remember God says YES! The two of you have given me a reason to live. You are my most prized possessions and I am completely honored to be your mother. I know that if everyone on this earth decided to turn their back on me I know that my two boys will still need me. You're entire lives are dependent upon me and the decisions I make as your mother and I promise you I will do my best to always make you proud. I'm not saying that life is going to be easy. I'm not saying we won't have our moments as we all continue to live. But know that mommy will always be here for you. No matter what. I want you to take your educations seriously and remember to dream big. Don't be afraid to follow those dreams because guess what: DREAMS DO COME TRUE! If they didn't you wouldn't be reading this note right now. I love you guys with every fiber of my being.

To my sister girls: Aisha Smith and Mapletine "Tina" Braswell. You two girls have become more than just friends. You are my sisters. You not only tell me the things that I want to hear, but you tell me the things that I don't want to hear. That is the true meaning of a friend. Just like siblings sometimes, we want to slap each other, but the love and admiration I have for both of you women of God is undeniable. Thank you for always being there. I've learned so much from the two of you and for these things, I am grateful to God for putting you in my life. I love you boos!!

To my In-laws thank you so much for accepting me into your family with open arms. I truly appreciate the love and support. It's an honor to be a Morgan.

To my childhood friend, Keyonna Stith: girl we go way back like Cadillac. Although we don't see each other, much, you know you'll always be my bff! It's been 20+ years and can't nobody take that away from us. I've watched you grow and mature into being an independent and responsible woman and one hell of a mother. Keep doing your thing, boo!

I also want to thank all of my friends and supporters from Arts High School. Class of two-five FOREVER!

To my two friends I've become so close to within these last couple of years, Shakeira Summers and Eddwina Gregg: I never thought that I would meet people in my adult life that I could truly trust and genuinely consider a friend. You two young women are amazing. I am so happy to have you in my life. Shakeira, thanks so much for all of your support in every single thing I do. You are truly my right hand and it's been an absolute pleasure to have you in my life. Eddy, I look up to you in so many ways. You are such an inspiration to simply do better. I pray that as I continue to grow as a businesswoman I gain just half of the knowledge that you posses. It is truly an honor to have you in my life.

I want to send a special thank you to my mentor since elementary school, D'Juana Smith. You are one of the realest people I know and you just DON'T AGE! Thank you so much for all of your love and guidance throughout the years. YOU ARE SUPERWOMAN!!

I want to thank my city of Newark, New Jersey also known as Brick City and my hood Hyatt Court Projects down in the Ironbound section of Newark for breeding a hustler on the streets and a boss in the boardrooms. They said "down bottom girls" would never be nothing. They threw us to the wolves down there and expected all of us to be eaten alive in these mean streets. They kept us down there with the toxins and the warehouses leaving us to rot. But I AM THE ROSE THAT GREW FROM CONCRETE! I want all of you to know that you too can make your dreams come true. Don't give up! I know life can get rough. I know reality in the hood ain't always filled with bright lights, flower fields, and peaches and cream but never allow your current situation determine your future. There is light after darkness and life after death.

To my spiritual family Pentecost Inspirational Baptist Church. I want to thank you all for your continued prayers and accepting me as apart of your family. In the midst of my dark hours you all never judged or shunned me . You continued to feed me the word of God and you loved me unconditionally. I love each and every one of you for that.

To my extended family I want to thank those of you who bullied me too. All of the fat names and the fat jokes only made me stronger. And to those of you who have supported me throughout the years with my music or other projects thank you so much. I know who you are and you know who you are.

To my AWESOME family in the Atlanta. You guys are always so supportive of me even from afar. Auntie Paula and Auntie NeNe I often pray that my marriage will last as long as yours. Thanks for being awesome examples of great women and wives. You little ladies roll with the punches and you throw a mean one too! I know where I get my crazy from! LOL. To my uncles Mill and Troy as well as my often-absent uncles Eddie and Bill, I love you all. While I don't get a chance to see you very often I know that you all love and support me. To Uncle Mill thanks so much for the sometimes-lengthy talks, words of encouragement and advice. You are such a wise man and I am truly grateful to have you in my life.

Uncle Troy thanks so much for your drunk nights and conversations and attempts to be my manager. You were one of the very first people to help me truly realize the power my voice had when I made you cry after singing your favorite song "Soon as I get home" by Faith Evans.

(can we please retire that song now? I'm not singing it at any more family functions! LOL.)

Uncle Bill and Uncle Eddie you two are truly busy bees. Thanks for showing me (and all of your nieces and nephews) what true hustlers really are. You guys are always on the go and taking care of your business but you find time to keep up with my latest endeavors and I appreciate that.

As the oldest grandchild on one side and the ONLY grandchild on the other I always felt pressure to succeed. To my first cousins.

Kendra I am so proud of the woman you have become. You're beautiful, smart, and independent! Keep up the great work! To my little cousin and my twin, Mama Love you are talented in so many ways. I want you to stay focused and keep your academics first! And always remember: to KEEP IT CUTE BOO!!! To Buggy I am a true believer in second chances and dude God has given you a second chance. Don't screw this up. You are such an intelligent young man and I can't wait to see your success once you begin to fully apply yourself. You are going to be unstoppable. I KNOW IT! To those Brumfield boys (Little Troy and Jordan) I love you guys! Thanks for showing my boys what its like to get roughed up a little. They need older cousins to boss them around a little and make them tough. You guys are also smart and gifted. Now one of ya'll hurry up and join the NFL! And don't forget I'm still the oldest and I'll still kick your butt!! HAHA!!

To my crazy estranged cousin in the military. You know who you are. All I'm gone say it I LOVE YOU ANYWAY!!

Last but certainly not least I want to thank the matriarchs of my family. To Grandma Brenda I want to thank you for keeping me in the house of God. Thank you for sitting me down night after night and instilling the word of God in me. The bible says, "train up a child in the way that he should go, and when he gets older he will not depart from it." I know who my help comes from and I am so honored to have a powerful woman of God as my grandmother. As the only child and therefore the only grandchild on your side thanks for keeping me spoiled!! * **Smile** *

Through the years you have kept me encouraged at times when I felt like I didn't even want to live anymore. I don't know what I'd do without you and only God knows where I'd be if it weren't for you. I love you!

To Grandma Tu-Tu. Thank you for being a prime example of a woman not allowing her fat to be her flaw. I can honestly say that I've never once heard you complain about your weight in my life! You are probably the biggest woman I know yet you exude confidence. You've never let yourself go. To this very day you still can put it on and step out looking better then most of these younger women. I pray that God continues to keep his healing hands on your body because you have lots more to do on this Earth young lady! Thanks for the endless comeback jokes during the years I was bullied. It helped me get through a lot of days when I just wanted to give up. I love you so much. Thank You!

PROFESSIONAL ACKNOWLEDGMENTS

I want to start by thanking my amazing Glam Squad for creating the awesome cover images and promo images for this project. To my amazingly multi-talented photographer Tahir Coleman Photography thank you so much for bringing your expertise and talents to this project. I also want to thank you for all of the EXTRA that you do. You helped me make one of my dreams come true. I can't even repay you for that. Thank you so much. To my talented hair stylist Aisha Jordan boo you have done your thing once again. Thanks for ALWAYS going above and beyond the call of duty. You are truly an artist and hair is your canvas. I've never been able to trust a hair stylist the way I trust you. Thanks for always making me look amazing. Not just for this project but on the regular!

To Ms. Khadijah Sumnter of Beat-YOU-tiful Makeup Artistry your skill, professionalism, and determination is admirable. Thank you so much for making me FLAWLESS honey! You are truly amazing! Remember to always believe in yourself, even when others don't. I also want to send a shout out to Glam Hair Beauty Bar for the amazing fantasy hair you see on the cover!

Next I'd like to thank the women of my organization, my baby, Elite Plus Incorporated. Felecia Crute, Latasha Briggs, Aja Johnson, Kenya Amons, Cara King, and Alreema Vinging you ladies are truly amazing. I appreciate all of the hard work you have put into my first baby, Elite Plus Inc. I am only as strong as my

103

team and I can confidently say my team is the BEST! Aside from being awesome team members you all are beautiful women on the inside and out and great friends. I look forward to the growth in our personal lives as well as within Elite Plus.

To the other plus positive organizations and to the entire plus community including but not limited to bloggers, magazines, major events that take place across the country, boutiques, buyers, models, etc. thank you for dedicating your lives to showing the world just how awesome we are! If it weren't for you there would be no me!

To my secret weapon Kim McCarter, CEO of Born Social, thank you so much for your assistance in branding this project. I must admit...you know your stuff!! What I love about you is you are never afraid to think outside the box! And you keep me on my toes! We need more people like you in this industry. Just don't forget about us little people when you blow up!

I also want to thank my proofreader Femi Lewis. I also want to thank authors W. Roger Brownlee also known as Professor of Plump Fiction and D'Juana Smith. You've both made yourselves available to me when I had tons of questions about this new endeavor. Thank You.

I also want to thank Ev Spaulding of JoanArk Pro for helping me with a lot of my graphic design needs not only for this project but for Elite Plus Inc. as well.

Last but not least I want to thank you. I don't know if you purchased this book just to be nosey, just to get up in my business, to have something to talk about or if you truly wanted to support me and you believe in the movement. Either way I want to thank you for taking time out of your lives to read this book. Because of you one of my dreams have come true. So pat yourself on the back! You deserve it!

ABOUT THE AUTHOR

"I AM WHAT GOD SAYS I AM"

Open. Honest. Outspoken. And Respectful. Tro-Jah Irby-Morgan learned the importance of possessing these characteristics at an early age. She can recall her mom always encouraging her to "say what's on your mind, but do it respectfully." The ability to stand up for herself and what she believed in is what has catapulted her into an abundance of success and accomplishments at such an early age.

A star was born March 18, 1987 to two of the most hard working people on this Earth, Marcus Irby and Felecia Crute. Tro-Jah was surrounded by examples of what can happen when you work hard as well as the repercussions of making the wrong choices. Her early years provided a glimpse of struggles being raised in a

Newark, NJ Housing Project by her mother. Growing up her father was in and out of penitentiaries but his presence was always known.

At the tender age of two, Tro-Jah's mother discovered her belting out R&B sensation Karyn White's song, "Superwoman." At that moment her mother knew she had a gift from God. Raised in the church Tro-Jah began singing in the choir. Often she was pressured to impromptu performances at family functions and Tro-Jah couldn't stand it. But she knew you had to be ready because you never know who's watching and listening. Always the biggest student in class and the biggest kid in the family, Tro-Jah was a victim of bullying. Not just in school but within her extended family. For years Tro-Jah struggled with confidence and self-esteem issues due to her weight. But she never allowed it to stop her from pursuing her dreams.

"I am...what God says I am" became her mantra. Even during her bullying years some of her peers and authoritative figures would see she had the natural ability to lead. It all started after being elected student council president in middle school, a leader on the basketball team, cheerleading, and the pep squad during her high school years. Not only did she excel in her talent she excelled academically as well. She was accepted into the gifted and talented program in the 7th grade at University High school. She went on to audition and be accepted into the famed Arts High School in Newark, NJ. During those years she broke barriers by being the ONLY plus sized girl in several pageants and took home the titles "Miss Essex County Talented Teen" and "Miss Christian Teen." She's also won the title of "Newark Idol." Tro-Jah went on to become a contestant on shows such as Showtime *At the Apollo, McDonald's Gospel Fest, BET's Sunday Best, The Voice,* and even *American Idol.* During those years, personal struggles reared its ugly head within her home. Tro-Jah's mom became addicted to drugs leaving Tro-Jah to fend for herself at the tender age of 15.

After graduating from Arts High School Tro-Jah began her academic journey in higher education. Tro-Jah's mother, who has now been sober for seven years, began her journey through rehabilitation. While education has been and will always be important to Tro-Jah, she decided to take another route after meeting the love of her life, Shameek Morgan and having her first child, Jahmeek. Music has always and will always be Tro-Jah's passion. She's had the honor of performing with amazing artists such as Rah Digga, Naughty by Nature, Leela James, Freddie Jackson, Melba Moore, Natalie Wilson, Cissy Houston, Vicki Winans, Hezekiah Walker, Trinity 5:7 and others.

After constantly being judged by her weight and not her talent in the music industry Tro-Jah's confidence slipped from little to none.

During her school years she realized that there was nothing for her outside of musical school activities. Tro-Jah always admired her mother's business sense and her father's hustler mentality. Tro-Jah knew one day she would also be a businesswoman. She didn't know what, when, or how but she knew the why. Tro-Jah wanted to create a space for plus size women and teen girls did not have a performing talent. She realized that demographic did not have an outlet. During a conversation with her husband in April of 2009 Elite Plus Incorporated was born. Elite Plus Inc. is a collective of plus size women who all share the common goal of empowering and encouraging women and teens in the plus size community. They celebrate their curves by hosting and attending different social and educational events. Since the company's launch in 2009 and its relaunch in July 2011 after the birth of her second child, Josiah, her second child Josiah Morgan) Elite Plus has had several successful events helping women identify their inner and outer beauty. Elite Plus has also had amazing supporters and has worked side by side with esteemed women in the plus size industry such as Gwen DeVoe, the creator of Full Figured Fashion Week; Shanda Freeman, fashion designer and co-star of MTV's *Man & Wife; and,* Famous Plus Model Jeannie Ferguson. Even with the success of these events this is only the beginning for the 25-year-old entrepreneur. In 2012 Tro-Jah also launched Diva Enterprise, LLC-a community incubator for outreach organizations and media. The purpose of Diva Enterprise is to empower and unite the plus community through events and social media. Diva Enterprise has several entities including "Diva+ Event Management", "Young Boss Lady Society", Elite Plus, and her first book "My Fat is Not a Flaw" published by her very own publishing company Diva Enterprise Books. Tro-Jah Irby-Morgan is a young woman is helping to empower, unite, and transform women. Her goal is to be a mogul for Generation Y (the Millennial Generation) and she is well on her way all because she is....what God says she is.

www.My FAT is NOT a Flaw.com

CPSIA information can be obtained
at www.ICGtesting.com
Printed in the USA
LVOW10s1554170118
563093LV00002B/148/P